This book belongs to:

____

____

Site	Username	Password

Site	Username	Password

Site	Username	Password

Site	Username	Password

Site	Username	Password

Site	Username	Password

Site	Username	Password

Site	Username	Password

Site	Username	Password

Site	Username	Password

Site	Username	Password

Site	Username	Password

Site	Username	Password

Site	Username	Password

Site	Username	Password

Site	Username	Password

Site	Username	Password

Site	Username	Password

Site	Username	Password

Site	Username	Password

Site	Username	Password

Site	Username	Password

Site	Username	Password

Site	Username	Password

Site	Username	Password

Site	Username	Password

Site	Username	Password

Site	Username	Password

Site	Username	Password

Site	Username	Password

Site	Username	Password

Site	Username	Password

Site	Username	Password

If you enjoy
using this book
please leave us your
opinion review. We
would enjoy hearing
from you and it helps
us create better books.
Peace out!

Made in the USA
Monee, IL
07 July 2026